B is for Bookworm

A Library Alphabet

Written by Anita C. Prieto and Illustrated by Renée Graef

Sleeping Bear Press

310 North Main Street, Suite 300
Chelsea, MI 48118
www.sleepingbearpress.com

© 2005 Thomson Gale, a part of the Thomson Corporation.

Thomson, Star Logo and Sleeping Bear Press are trademarks
and Gale is a registered trademark used herein under license.

Printed and bound in Canada.

10 9 8 7 6 5 4 3 2 1

Library of Congress Cataloging-in-Publication Data

Prieto, Anita C., 1933-
B is for bookworm : a library alphabet / written by Anita C. Prieto ;
illustrated by Renée Graef.
  p. cm.
ISBN 1-58536-145-3
1. Libraries—Juvenile literature. 2. Books—Juvenile literature. 3. English
language—Alphabet—Juvenile literature. I. Graef, Renée, ill. II. Title.
Z665.5.P75 2005
027—dc22   2005006024

For Deanna, Floyd, Lorraine, and Frank, for their encouragement and support...
and for my educational consultants, Christel, Judee, and Vertilee.

ANITA

❧

For the Madison Avenue and Center Street Book Club.

RENÉE

A is for Author

There are thousands of books on the library shelves,
just waiting for you and me.
They were written by people who love to create.
Do you know who those people might be?

A
a

The next time you go to the library, look around. You're surrounded by thousands of books. Every book was written by someone who wanted to tell a story. That person is called the author.

Authors write all kinds of books—fiction, nonfiction, biographies, plays, etc. Over 2,500 years ago, a Greek scholar named Aesop (e-sop) wrote hundreds of fables; stories with a lesson. Maybe you've read *The Ant and the Grasshopper*, one of his most famous fables. Have you heard of Mark Twain's *Tom Sawyer* or *Huckleberry Finn*? Children all over the world have loved the stories of Hans Christian Andersen (*The Ugly Duckling*), the Brothers Grimm (*Snow White and the Seven Dwarfs*), and Dr. Seuss (*The Cat in the Hat*). Good stories can last lifetimes. More than 400 years ago William Shakespeare wrote dozens of plays, including *Romeo and Juliet*, that are still enjoyed today.

After you've read a good story, have you ever thought, "I wish I could write like that." Well, give it a try! Your book can be anything you want it to be. That's the nice thing about writing a book. You, the author, decide what goes in it.

Illustration of author Anita Prieto

A bookworm is someone who loves to read. Benjamin Franklin was a bookworm. During his life he was a printer, an author, a librarian, a statesman, and an inventor. Ben Franklin collected books. But books were expensive, and most people couldn't afford to own them. So Franklin and some of his friends started the Leather Apron Club. They gave the club that name because they were printers, carpenters, blacksmiths, silversmiths, and candle and soap makers—they wore leather aprons when they worked to protect their clothing.

The Leather Apron Club members bought lots of books, and in 1731 they opened the first subscription lending library. People became members of the library by paying a fee of 40 shillings to join and 10 shillings each year. Forty shillings was a lot of money at that time, but that didn't stop people from joining the library. Thanks to Ben Franklin, his friends, and the lending library, more people could enjoy books.

Bb

B is for Bookworm

A bookworm gobbles up book after book.
When she's reading them, time really flies.
As she closes one book, she picks up another,
'cause each holds a different surprise.

The first public library in America may have been established in Charleston, South Carolina, in 1698 when the colonists passed an act "to secure the Provincial Library of Charlestown." The act allowed townspeople to "have liberty to borrow any book out of the said Provincial Library, giving a receipt."

The first libraries in Canada weren't community libraries. Instead, they were private collections, which early settlers brought with them from Europe. *The Canadian Encyclopedia* reports that "the first known library belonged to Marc Lescarbot, a scholar and advocate who came to Port-Royal in 1606." The same reference also reports that "the first free tax-supported (Canadian) public libraries date from 1883 and were in Saint John, Guelph, and Toronto."

In 1901 Andrew Carnegie, another bookworm, gave over five million dollars of his large fortune to build 65 branch libraries in New York City—libraries that would be free to everyone. Carnegie also gave money to open more than 100 libraries in Canada. As time went on, more and more free libraries were opened.

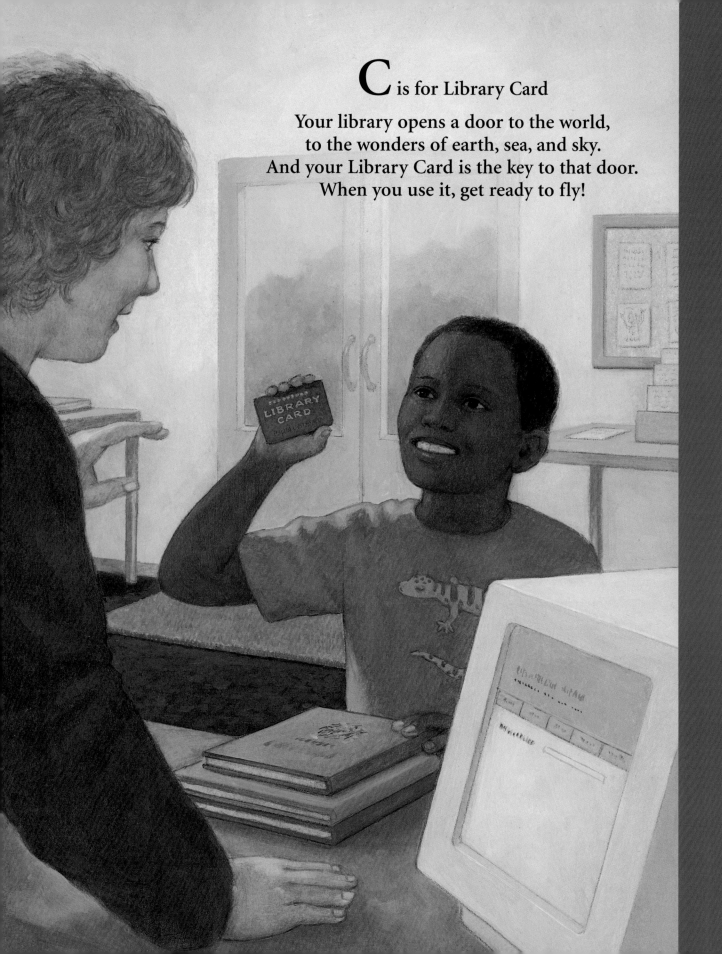

C is for Library Card

Your library opens a door to the world,
to the wonders of earth, sea, and sky.
And your Library Card is the key to that door.
When you use it, get ready to fly!

You need a key to enter your house each day. Without it, you'd be locked out. Well, the same thing is true when you use the public library. Anyone can visit the library, look through books on the shelves, read the magazines and newspapers, and use the reference materials. But in order to take home an item, you need something that will allow you to make full use of the library's resources. That "something" is a library card.

With your library card you become a member or "patron" of the library, a person who supports and uses the library. You can use your card at the neighborhood public library and at other public libraries in your town. Best of all, it's free. Public libraries are supported by local, state, and federal money, and also by donations.

Each September the American Library Association celebrates National Library Card Sign-Up Month. But you don't have to wait until then to become a library patron. Ask your librarian. You can join today!

000 GENERAL KNOWLEDGE
100 PHILOSOPHY Psychology
200 RELIGIONS Mythology
300 Social Sciences FOLKLORE
400 LANGUAGES Grammar
500 Mathematics NATURAL SCIENCES
600 Medicine TECHNOLOGY
700 ARTS Recreation
800 Literature
900 GEOGRAPHY HISTORY

D is for Dewey

If all of the books on the library shelves
were just placed anywhere—what a mess!
How in the world would you find the right book
when all you could do was just guess?

Melvil Dewey was only 21 years old when he invented the Dewey Decimal Classification System. He was working as a student assistant in the Amherst College Library in Massachusetts. At that time, library books weren't organized in any official way. Some librarians arranged them on shelves alphabetically, by the author's last name. Other librarians had different systems. If you were looking for a book about a certain subject, you might have to look in 10 different places all around the library.

Dewey thought that was a terrible waste of time and effort. He invented the Dewey Decimal Classification System, a system that sorts books into 10 large categories. Then he encouraged librarians all over the country to use his system. Once that happened, it was much easier to find a book.

Melvil Dewey worked to improve libraries all his life. He helped to establish the American Library Association, he opened the first library school at Columbia College in New York City, and he encouraged women to become librarians at a time when libraries were staffed mostly by men. He is often called the "Father of Modern Librarianship."

Dd

A book is a collection of information, a way to preserve knowledge. Even before there were books as we know them today, people wanted to preserve knowledge.

The people of ancient Mesopotamia saved information on clay tablets. A scribe (someone who knew how to write) used a pointed instrument called a stylus to form wedge-shaped symbols in the softened clay. Then the clay was baked until it was hard and dry. This early writing is called cuneiform (ku-ne-a-form), which means "wedge-shaped."

Ancient Egyptians used a kind of picture-writing called hieroglyphics (hi-er-o-glif-iks). The Egyptians wrote on papyrus, an early form of paper. Our word "paper" comes from the word *papyrus*. The Egyptians took reeds from the papyrus plant, slit them open, and pounded them together. When the reeds dried, they formed long "writing sheets" called scrolls. Once the scrolls were covered with information, they were rolled up and stored in large clay jars or in boxes made of wood and ivory.

It wasn't until paper was used for recording and saving information that there were books like the ones we use today.

E e

E is for Early Books

If there were no notebooks to use in school,
no pencils when you had to write,
how would you copy your new spelling words
to take home and study each night?

Ff

In libraries there are two broad categories of books: Fiction and Nonfiction.

Fiction books contain stories that aren't true: The stories were created or made up. Fiction books can take you to exciting places all over the world, and to even more exciting places in make-believe worlds all over the universe. Fiction books are arranged alphabetically, according to the author's last name. For example, if you are looking for *Little Women* by Louisa May Alcott, look for a book with "ALC" printed on the spine.

Nonfiction books are filled with facts and information. They might be about real people, real places, and real things. Fact: *B is for Bookworm* is a nonfiction book that gives you information about libraries. Suppose you want to know where the Wright brothers flew their first airplane and how they did it. Or maybe you are curious about how a caterpillar turns into a beautiful butterfly. In both cases, nonfiction is the place to go.

Fiction or nonfiction. Which will it be? It all depends on what you are looking for.

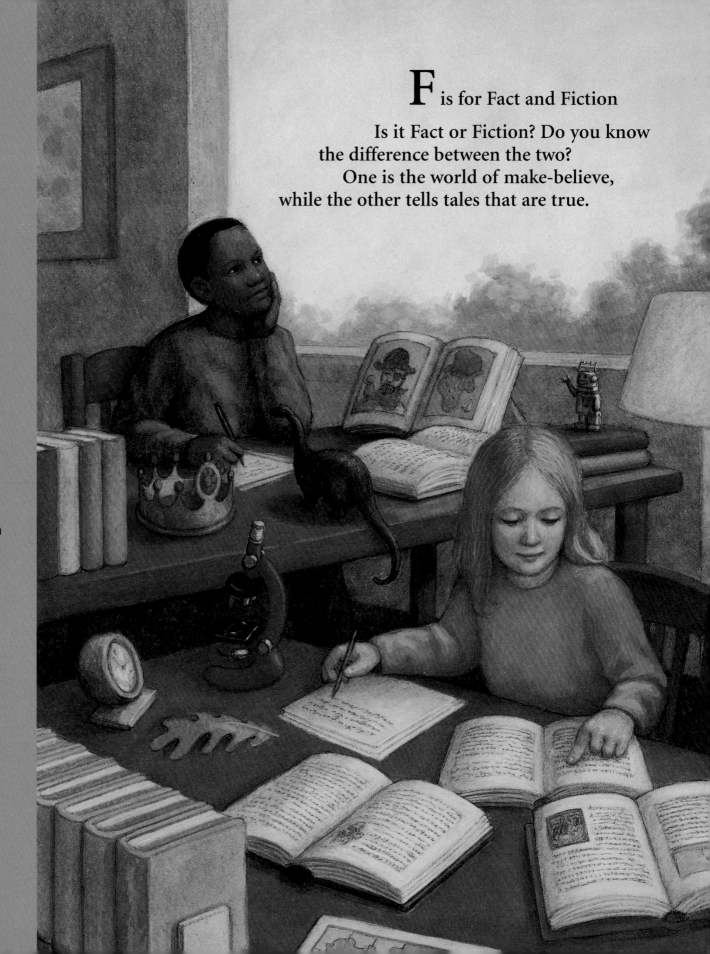

F is for Fact and Fiction

Is it Fact or Fiction? Do you know
the difference between the two?
One is the world of make-believe,
while the other tells tales that are true.

G is for Gutenberg

Would you like to copy your history book,
all 322 pages?
That's what you'd do if you were a scribe
and lived in the Middle Ages.

During the Middle Ages, books were rare and expensive because each one had to be copied by hand. In monasteries monks worked in silence copying religious writings. It took many months, even years to copy one book.

Another way to copy a book was to carve words into a block of wood, cover the block with ink, and then press the wood block onto a sheet of paper. Under pressure, the ink on the wood block was transferred onto the paper. But each page of the book had to be carved into a separate block of wood, and that was time-consuming and difficult to do.

Johannes Gutenberg changed printing forever. Born in Germany around 1397, Gutenberg worked as a goldsmith. He devised a way to make individual letters out of metal. Then he arranged the letters to compose a page in a book. He inked a simple hand press and printed the page. Once that page was printed Gutenberg rearranged the metal letters to compose the next page of the book. His was the first movable-type printing press.

Compare Gutenberg's methods with modern-day "electronic printing" where an entire book can be saved on one computer disk and a copy made with the touch of a printer's button. What a difference!

H is for Historic

Some library buildings are very new.
Some library buildings are old.
But look inside and what you will find
are treasures more precious than gold.

Historic means "of great importance in history." The Library of Alexandria in Egypt, built over two thousand years ago, is of great importance to library history.

Egyptian Pharaoh Ptolemy I (Tol-uh-mee) was a curious man who not only wanted to learn about his own people but also wanted to understand people living in other countries. He ordered a Greek scholar, Demetrius of Phalerum, to gather a collection of manuscripts from various countries. His successors, Ptolemy II and Ptolemy III, continued his work, and this library grew. It had sections on mathematics, astronomy, science, geometry, and medicine. How the Library of Alexandria was destroyed is a mystery, but many historians believe it was destroyed by fire almost two thousand years ago.

Today, a new library, the Bibliotheca Alexandrina, has been built overlooking the Mediterranean Sea at Alexandria's Eastern Harbor. When it opened, the library had 200,000 books. It will eventually house over eight million books.

I i

I is for Illustrations

When you open a book and the pictures appear
with a rainbow of colors so bright,
you'll probably shout, as you check that book out,
"Hey! I'm reading this one tonight."

Have you heard the saying, "One picture is worth 1,000 words?" Think about it. If you were asked to describe a picture of the signing of the Declaration of Independence, could you do it in one word? Or even one sentence? Probably not. If you wanted to tell the whole story of what the picture shows, it might take a thousand words or even more. Yet one picture tells it all.

An illustrator is the person who draws the pictures you see in books or magazines. Some pictures in books are photographs, but, more than likely, you'll find a drawn picture, an illustration. Illustrations help explain the text, the written part, of a book. Often they show what is happening in the story. Sometimes they even show additional details not found in the written text. But, most of all, illustrations add to the beauty of any book.

Do you have a favorite illustrated book? Perhaps you love *Where the Wild Things Are* by Maurice Sendak or maybe you think Chris Van Allsburg's *The Polar Express* is the greatest. No matter what your favorite is, illustrations really make a story come alive.

J is for Juvenile Books

Some books are scary, some make you laugh,
   some teach you lessons, that's true.
But never forget, if you look hard enough,
   there's a book out there made just for you.

Everyone loves a good book, but you wouldn't give a baby an encyclopedia, would you? That's why, when you walk into a library or bookstore, you'll find all kinds of books for people of all ages. Juvenile books are made specifically for children to read.

Board books and Cloth books are printed especially for babies. They are small, brightly colored, and easy for tiny fingers to handle. Some have fuzzy pictures for babies to touch and feel. Concept books are "learning books." Using them, toddlers learn about the alphabet, numbers, colors, shapes, animals, and other things. Picture books tell a story using beautiful illustrations. Some picture books are very simple with only a word or two on each page, while others tell a longer story. Beginning Readers books, like *One Fish Two Fish Red Fish Blue Fish*, have a simple vocabulary with much repetition to help young readers to learn.

As children grow and become better readers, they move to Chapter books, which are longer and have fewer pictures. Teenagers enjoy more complicated Young Adult books.

No matter what your age, there's a book out there just waiting for you to enjoy.

Jj

k
k
K

There are special places and tools within the library that can help make it easier for you to use all of its resources. Look for these places on your next visit to your library.

Without the Card Catalog, finding information in the library would be very difficult. In some libraries, the Card Catalog is a large cabinet holding a file of hundreds of cards, one for each library item. The cards are arranged alphabetically by author, title, and subject, and tell the patron where to locate an item. Now, with the use of computers, many libraries have databases or Online catalogs that contain all of that information.

Archives hold special collections of records. Public records and historical documents are kept in archives. An archive might contain the personal papers of an individual, or photographs, pamphlets, and even news-paper clippings.

K is for Knowing

Some library places hold special things,
and it helps to know just where to look.
The bigger you grow, the more you should know
when you check out a library book.

The Circulation Desk (or Check-Out Desk) is the place where books are checked out or returned to a library. If you don't return a book on time, it is also the place to pay the overdue fines.

The Stacks are where books are shelved. In small libraries you can walk through the stacks and select your own book. In very large libraries, a librarian might go into the stacks to get a book for you.

The Vertical File is a large cabinet or drawer that holds items of unusual shape or size. It's where librarians store large pictures, newspaper clippings, brochures, and pamphlets.

The Library of Congress, in Washington, D.C., has over 29 million books and other printed materials, and that's only part of its total collection. There are also huge collections of maps, photographs, films, manuscripts, musical recordings, and many other things, including the handwritten copy of Lincoln's Gettysburg Address. According to one expert, "it is the largest collection of knowledge in the world." It is open to the public and its collections are housed in three connected buildings—the Thomas Jefferson, John Adams, and James Madison buildings.

The Founding Fathers knew the importance of knowledge and wanted the members of Congress to have as much information as possible at their fingertips. In 1800 they established the Library of Congress. There were 740 books and three maps in the first collection.

During the War of 1812, British soldiers burned the Capitol Building. All of the Library of Congress books were lost. Fortunately, Founding Father Thomas Jefferson offered to sell his personal book collection to Congress to rebuild this national treasure. Today, important documents are scanned into electronic files so they can never be lost again.

L l

L is for Library of Congress

The Library of Congress is one of the sights
you might visit in Washington, D.C.
It has thousands of pictures and millions of books.
It is something you surely should see.

M is for Media Center

Everything changes from day to day,
nothing stays quite the same.
When you visit your library, you may find
that it now has a brand-new name.

At one time, the library was all about books. Maybe there were some maps there, or even a few magazines. But mostly you'd find books. That's no longer true. Libraries have changed to keep up with the changing times and changing technology. Today libraries are often called media centers, and librarians are called media specialists.

Audiovisual media refers to films, cassette tapes, compact disks, videotapes, and other audiovisual materials used to record information.

Books, magazines, and newspapers are part of the print media category.

Computers, too, have changed the way libraries function. Teaching research and technology skills is now an important part of every librarian's program. And, as you read earlier, online catalogs found in computers have every bit of library information stored in a giant database, available to you with the click of a mouse. What a great improvement!

Call numbers are part of the Dewey Decimal System. They make the librarian's job a little easier. Once you understand call numbers, finding a book will be easy for you, too. A call number is written on the spine of every book. Some call numbers are just letters. Some are a combination of letters and numbers. This is how they work.

Think of the library as a giant city made of books. In this "city" there are many "neighborhoods" called Easy Books, Fiction, Nonfiction, Reference Books, Juvenile Books, etc. Now in each neighborhood, pretend the bookshelves are streets. Each book is a house on a particular street. When you look up a book in the card catalog, look for its call number. It will give you the "address" of the book and tell you exactly on what "street" that book lives. If the call number says "F," look in the Fiction neighborhood. "R" means look in the Reference neighborhood. If there are numbers in the call number, look in the Nonfiction neighborhood. Check out the following examples:

F
SEW
Fiction: *Black Beauty*
by Anna Sewell

R
032
NEW
Reference: *New Encyclopaedia Britannica*

Call numbers make using the library easy. Ask your librarian for help if you need it.

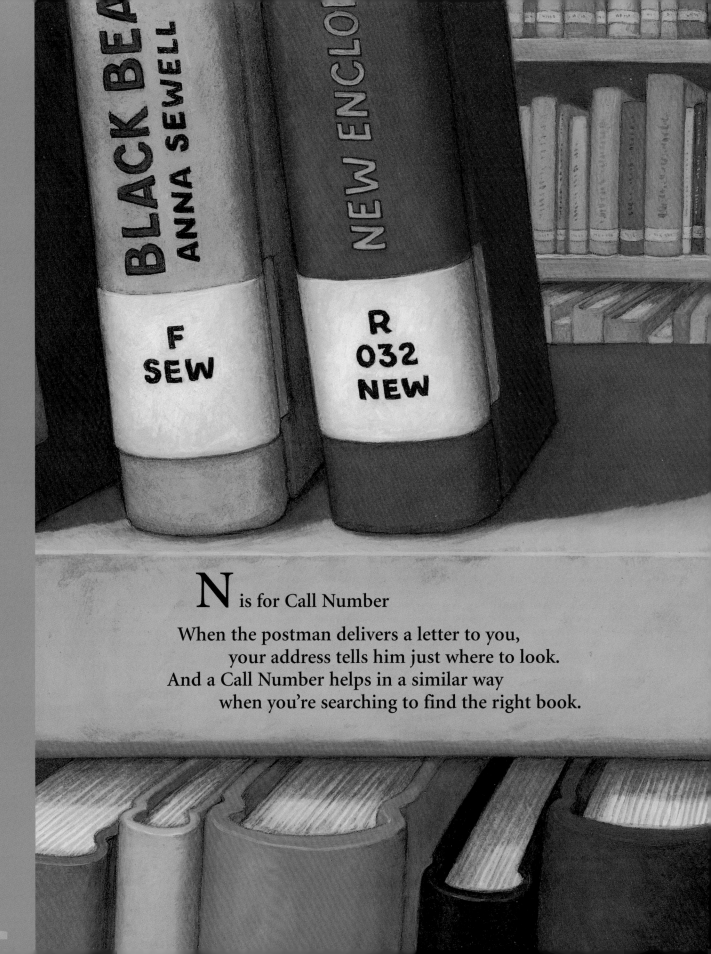

N is for Call Number

When the postman delivers a letter to you,
your address tells him just where to look.
And a Call Number helps in a similar way
when you're searching to find the right book.

O is for Online

Our language is living, it changes and grows;
some words may die out, others stay.
"Online" is a new word that you'll want to learn
when using computers each day.

PLEASE REGISTER
AT THE FRONT DESK
BEFORE USING COMPUTER.

When your grandmother was a little girl, a "computer" was an adding machine, a "mouse" was a creature she chased out of her kitchen, and "online" was a place to hang newly washed laundry to dry in the sun. Today those words and their meanings may have changed.

These days computers are everywhere, helping us in hundreds of ways. Computers hold a giant database filled with information. A database is an organized collection of facts. Your telephone book is a database, an organized collection of names and telephone numbers. The online library catalog is a database, too.

When you use the computer as a research tool, you'll need to go online. "Online" means being connected to the Internet, which is an electronic communications network linked to other computer networks around the world. (Remember, always get your parents' permission before going online.) Once online, you select a "search engine," a program used to search out facts. Maybe you've heard of search engines called "Google," "AltaVista," or "Ask Jeeves." "Yahooligans" is a search engine specially designed for kids.

Did you know that you could also read books online? E-books are electronic versions of books delivered through your computer by E-publishing—electronic publishing. You can read your e-book on your computer screen or download it into a special handheld reader.

Oo

P is for Presidential Libraries

The President's job keeps him busy all day
doing everything that is required.
    Signing letters and papers and dozens of laws,
I'll bet that his fingers get tired!

P p

Presidential libraries have a special purpose:
to preserve important documents and
papers collected during the administration
of a president of the United States.

Before the presidential library system was
begun, important presidential papers were
not kept in one place. Some were sent to
historical societies. Others were kept in
private collections. Some were lost or
destroyed. People realized that this wasn't
a good way to preserve history. So in 1939,
President Franklin Roosevelt presented all
of his presidential papers to the federal
government. The Franklin D. Roosevelt
Presidential Library was dedicated and
opened in 1941.

Every president since Roosevelt has done
the same thing. Today there is a national
network of libraries dedicated to housing
items that are part of our national heritage.
The libraries contain documents, photographs, audiotapes, videotapes, motion
picture films, etc... anything that will provide
a record of public policy during a president's
time in office.

The presidential library system is part of
the National Archives and Records
Administration. Presidential libraries are
located all across America in the state in
which each president lived. They are custo-
dians of large parts of American history
and open to the public.

A quest is a special search to find something important. Have you ever wondered
about who you are or how your family came
to live where they do? If so, you need to set
out on a genealogy quest. A genealogy quest
is a lot of fun. But here's a warning—once
you begin you may never want to stop!

Genealogy is the study of a family's pedigree,
a family's history. You can begin your genealogy quest by creating a family tree, which is
a written chart that shows you, your family,
and all the members of your family from one
generation to the next. The library is a good
place to find materials on how a family
tree is created.

Once you've read about the basics of genealogy, talk to your parents and other relatives
like grandparents, aunts, and uncles. Add
their names to your family tree.

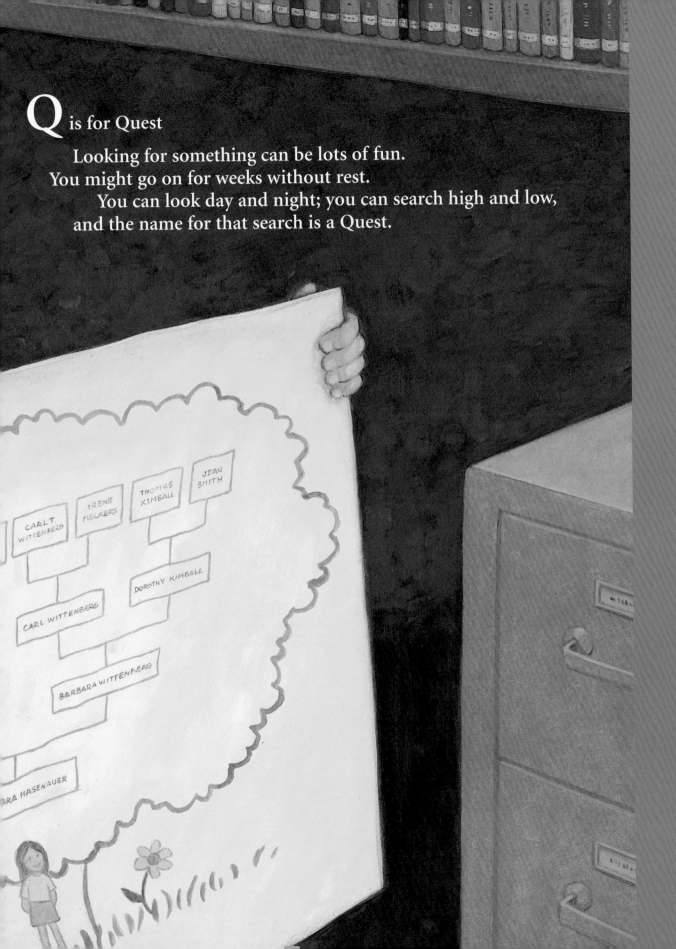

Q is for Quest

Looking for something can be lots of fun.
You might go on for weeks without rest.
You can look day and night; you can search high and low,
and the name for that search is a Quest.

Many families keep information such as birthdates and marriages in scrapbooks or other family records. You might even visit the cemetery to get names of relatives who are buried there. Finally, ask your relatives if anyone has been working to create a family tree. They'll be happy to share information.

Now go back to your library and look for the genealogy section. Old newspaper files, census records, and the city directory are gold mines of information. Ask about ship records and immigration lists. Unless you are a Native American, someone in the past, one of your ancestors, came to America as an immigrant. His name may be on a ship record just waiting to be found. All you need is an idea and the quest is on!

R is for Reference

Why is the moon always changing its shape
and how does the sun get its heat?
To answer your questions and get all the facts
a Reference book just can't be beat.

Reference books are nonfiction books that contain useful facts and information. When you need to write a report or do any research, you often will use a reference book. The call number for a reference book begins with R. Here are some examples of different reference books you can find at your local library.

An encyclopedia is a reference work consisting of many volumes. Information on a variety of topics is arranged alphabetically.

The atlas is a collection of maps in book form. You'll find maps of every country in an atlas.

An almanac is a reference manual published each year. It has tables showing a variety of useful information. One example of an almanac is *The Old Farmer's Almanac*, first published in 1792, and now published yearly in September. Farmers still consult it for weather forecasts, sunrise times, planting information, and other useful facts.

Usually, you can't check out a reference book; it stays in the library. However, there are online versions available, which you can access on your home computer.

R r

S is for Storytelling

When the Three Little Pigs met the Big Bad Wolf,
he just huffed and he puffed and he blew.
Well, the Storytime Lady knows what happened next,
and she's waiting to tell it to you.

S s

Libraries are excellent community resources. School librarians plan activities for students. Community librarians present programs for anyone who enjoys coming to the library.

Storytelling is one example of a community program. If you visit a community library most mornings, you'll find a group of happy toddlers sitting quietly and listening to stories being told (perhaps *The Three Little Pigs* or *Clifford the Big Red Dog*). Another group of children may be singing songs, reciting nursery rhymes, or watching a finger play. Older preschool children come to the library with their parents for story hour, to see films or puppet shows, and even to do arts and crafts.

Community libraries serve everyone. Children of all ages can take part in summer reading programs. Adults come to the library for special programs, too. Rooms are available for meetings and discussion groups. Guest speakers speak on a variety of topics. Authors present new books for discussion. College students meet to do research or study for exams. The library is a very busy place.

T is for Traveling Libraries

A donkey, a camel, and sometimes a boat
deliver a happy surprise.
And when these strange libraries come to town,
you will not believe your eyes.

In some parts of the world, if you can't go to the library, the library will come to you!

Kenya, a country on the African continent, has lots of sand and many unpaved roads. In some rural areas, cars or buses cannot be driven. The Kenya National Library Service created the Camel Library Service to take books to isolated villages. Twice a month, three camels set out to deliver books. One camel carries boxes of books. Another carries a tent and other supplies. The third camel is used as a spare.

In Zimbabwe, a country south of Kenya, Donkey Libraries bring more than books. The donkeys also pull Electro-Communication Library Carts, which can provide radio, telephone, e-mail, and Internet service when they visit remote communities. The carts have batteries charged by solar energy. The librarians are hoping to add satellite dishes some day to help villages network and share information.

In Norway and Sweden, book boats carry thousands of books each year to people who find it difficult to get to a regular library. In our own country bookmobiles are sent to small towns and places without libraries.

Tt

Uu

U is for Useful parts of a book

It's helpful to know all the parts of a book.
Your teacher will say, "Wow! You're clever!"
It just takes a moment to study their names,
and then you will know them forever.

Have you noticed how many parts there are to a book? Knowing what's inside (and outside) a book can be useful.

The **book cover** protects the **text**—which is everything inside the book—just as the **book jacket** protects the cover. The **spine** holds all the pages together. If the book is from a library, there will be a **call number** on the spine. The **title page** is the first thing you see when you open a book, and contains the names of the **author**, the **illustrator**, and the **publisher** (who printed the book).

On the back of the title page you will find the **ISBN** (International Standard Book Number). Librarians use this number to order the book. The ISBN for *B is for Bookworm* is 1-58536-145-3. Can you find it?

The **preface** is an introduction and tells you what the book is about. The **table of contents** is a list of chapters with their page numbers. At the back of the book you'll often find a **glossary**, an alphabetical list of definitions and pronunciations of unusual words used in the book. You may also find a **bibliography**, a list of other books you might want to read. The author puts extra information in the **appendix** at the end of the book. Finally, some books have an **index**, an alphabetical list of topics found in the book along with their page numbers.

The next time you pick up a book, see how many useful parts you can find!

B is for Bookworm
A Library Alphabet

Written by
Anita C. Prieto
Illustrated by
Renée Graef

CONTENTS

A IS FOR AUTHOR
B IS FOR BOOKWORM
C IS FOR LIBRARY CARD
D IS FOR DEWEY
E IS FOR EARLY BOOK
F IS FOR FACT OR FI
G IS FOR GUTENBE
H IS FOR HISTOR
I IS FOR ILLU
J IS FOR JI

Library of Congress Cataloging-in-Publication Data

Prieto, Anita C.,1953
B is for Bookworm: a library alphabet / Written by Anita C. Prieto
Illustrated by Renée Graef

p. cm.

ISBN 1-58536-145-3

1. Libraries–Juvenile Literature. 2. Books–Juvenile literature. 3. English language–Alphabet–Juvenile literature. I. Graef, Renée, ill. II. Title

Z665.5.P75 2005

027–dc22

2005006224

Your vocabulary is the total amount of words you know and use correctly. With a good vocabulary, you can explain things clearly and understand more of what you read. Reading improves your vocabulary because it introduces you to new words.

Using a thesaurus can improve your vocabulary. The thesaurus, a reference book, contains an alphabetical list of words and their synonyms (words that have the same or almost the same meaning). If you look up "earthquake" in a thesaurus, you'll find the synonyms temblor, seism, tremor, and quake.

The dictionary will also improve your vocabulary. It tells how a word is spelled. It gives a definition of the word. It shows how to divide a word into syllables. It also lists synonyms. Often a dictionary tells the origin of the word—that is, it tells you the "story" of how the word came into our language. Here's an example:

Long before paper was invented, people found ways to record ideas. Primitive Romans made a writing surface from the inner bark of *liber* trees. Over time, the name of this tree also came to mean "book." The Roman word *libraria* means "bookseller's shop." When that word entered the English language, it meant "a place for books." Knowing this, you can understand how our word "library" was born. Your local library has "word stories" like these and many more, all of which can improve your vocabulary!

V v

V is for Vocabulary

"How is the weather?" What would you say
to make sure your friend understood?
"It's raining! It's snowing! The storm winds are blowing."
Or would you just say, "It's not good."

Awards are given for many things, including books. Each year the American Library Association (ALA) awards the John Newbery Medal to the "author of the most distinguished contribution to American children's literature published in the preceding year." Newbery was an English bookseller who lived in the eighteenth century. The ALA also awards the Randolph Caldecott Medal to the "artist of the most distinguished American Picture Book for children..." Caldecott was a talented children's illustrator who lived in the nineteenth century.

Children's book awards are given in other countries, too. The Canadian Library Association (CLA) gives a medal each year for the best children's book published in Canada and written by a citizen or resident of Canada. The Canadian Association of Children's Librarians gives the Amelia Frances Howard-Gibbon Illustrator's Award yearly. Another Canadian award is the Governor-General's Award for Children's Literature.

W is for Winner

How would you feel if your name were called
and you heard, "You're the Winner today!"
Would you jump up and down and clap your hands?
Or stand up and shout "HOORAY!"

In Great Britain, the Carnegie Medal is given yearly to an outstanding book published in the United Kingdom. The Kate Greenaway Medal is given for the most distinguished work in the illustration of children's books published in the United Kingdom.

All of these awards are highly prized by children's authors and illustrators.

Sam the Dra[gon]

Max Laughner

JOHN NEWBERY MEDAL

THE CALDECOTT MEDAL

X is for Xylograph

You're probably thinking that blocks are just toys,
and today that is true, as a rule.
But long ago people in faraway lands
printed books using blocks as a tool!

A xylograph (zi-lo-graf) is an engraving on a wood block. *Xylo* comes from a Greek word meaning "wood." *Graph* comes from a Greek word meaning "writing." So a xylograph is writing on wood. That's another word story to add to your collection.

About two thousand years ago in Far Eastern countries, scholars developed a way to print. They took thick wooden blocks and carved pictures and letters in the wood. The images had to be carved in reverse so that when they were printed, they could be read. This wasn't an easy thing to do, especially if the work to be printed was long or complicated.

Perhaps you've seen the xylograph method used even today. Have you ever carved a picture into the large flat edge of a potato, dipped the potato into paint, and then "printed" a pattern on paper? If you did, you were imitating the ancient scholars of long ago. Strange as it may seem, xylographic printing is still used today in the country of Tibet, where Tibetan monks print manuscripts in this ancient manner.

X

X

Y is for Yellow

A ruby red rose or a bright blue sky
show us colors so lovely to see.
But yellow's the color librarians love,
'cause they wear it to get their degree.

The next time you attend a university graduation ceremony, look at the robes worn by the graduates as they march into the auditorium. While most are black, some have bright bands of color down the front. Each graduate receiving a master's (or advanced) degree wears a colored hood designating the school from which he is receiving his degree. Red, blue, green, purple—you'll see every color in the rainbow. You'll also see yellow, because when librarians receive their Master of Library Science degree, they wear the color yellow.

The American Library Association estimates there are more than 117,000 libraries in the United States—public libraries, academic libraries, school libraries, and business libraries. Opportunities for librarians are everywhere. Have you ever thought you might want to be a librarian? Ask yourself a few questions. Do you love books? Do you like to help people? Do you think it's fun to answer a lot of questions? Do you like to organize things?

If you answered "yes" to most of those questions, a librarian's job might just be perfect for you. You'll never be bored working in a library. There's always something new and exciting happening there.

Z is for Zestful

If you wake up smiling and you're full of Zest,
and you tackle the day, meeting every test,
when you just keep trying, and you never rest,
be proud of yourself, 'cause you're doing your best!

If you look up zestful in your dictionary, you'll see that it means "full of zest—stimulating and giving keen relish and hearty enjoyment." That's a pretty good description of your library. It's a place that leaves you a little happier whenever you visit. A place that makes you excited because you've uncovered an astonishing bit of information that simply blows your mind. Think about how happy you feel when you've found a certain book you've wanted to read for a long time. Or how happy you are to check out a movie you've been waiting to see. Zestful is a good word for a library.

Sometimes we get so used to something we take it for granted. Don't let that happen with your library. People throughout the ages have worked hard to create this special place. Use your library often. Take a friend with you. Even better, volunteer as a library aide and help others to acquire a zest for all the things the library offers. Just remember, once you've discovered your neighborhood library and met the librarian, you've found a lifelong friend!

Z z

Did You Know?

Fun Facts about Authors, Books, and of course, Libraries

1. Sometimes books are called volumes. The first "books" were papyrus rolls. The Latin word for "roll" is *volumen* and that's what they called these books.

2. A pseudonym (su-do-nim) is a name used by an author that is not his real name. "Mark Twain" is a pseudonym. Twain's real name is Samuel Langhorne Clemens. Dr. Seuss' real name is Theodor Seuss Geisel.

3. The citizens of Salisbury, Connecticut, claim to have established the first Children's Library. In 1803, a man named Caleb Bingham donated 150 books for children. This was the beginning of the Bingham Library for Youth.

4. When the American Library Association was formed in Philadelphia in 1876, there were 156 members and only 10 were women. Today the ALA is the largest library association in the world, with more than 64,000 members—men and women.

5. There is a National Library Symbol, a white silhouette of a person reading a book shown on a bright blue background. Have you seen one in your neighborhood?

6. There are 530 miles of bookshelves in the Library of Congress.

7. The first recorded librarian was Zenodotus of Ephesus, appointed by Ptolemy I.

8. In addition to presidential libraries, there are many other specialized libraries, including law libraries, music libraries, and medical libraries. There are even libraries where you can borrow tools! Need a pruning shears or a posthole digger? Check out the Friends of Sligo Creek Lending Library in Maryland. Need a hammer, a drill, or a ladder? The Tool Lending Library in Berkeley, California, is the place to go.

9. Not all books are found on a library shelf. There are many specialized "books" for people with physical handicaps. Talking books, found on disks and cassettes, bring much pleasure to the blind, as do books in Braille. There are large-print books for people with vision problems. A special television set will magnify and enlarge a page of text to make it easier to read. And a Kurzweil Machine changes printed text into the sound of speech.

10. When the Egyptians stored their scrolls, they placed a tag on the end of each scroll. The tag, called a *titulus* by the Romans, told what the scroll was about. From *titulus* came our word "title."

11. Johannes Gutenberg's first major printing job was the Bible, approximately 1,200 pages long.

12. In Medieval times, books were so rare and precious they were chained to the walls for safekeeping.

13. The Family History Library of the Church of Jesus Christ of Latter-day Saints was founded in 1894 to assist members in gathering genealogical records. The largest library of its kind in the world, its Ancestral File database contains over 35 million names. Records are available from all over the world. There may be a branch of the Family History Library in your town.

14. If you visit the John Hay Library at Brown University in Providence, Rhode Island, you can see some of the oldest "books" known to man—27 cuneiform tablets that came from ancient Mesopotamia.

15. Benjamin Franklin (Founding Father), Henry Wadsworth Longfellow (famous American poet), the Grimm Brothers (authors of wonderful stories for children), J. Edgar Hoover (once head of the F.B.I.), Laura Bush (wife of the 43rd president of the United States), and Bat Girl (comic strip heroine) all have something in common. At one time in their lives, they were all librarians!

"I would also have in every library a friend of the young, whom they can consult freely when in want of assistance, and who, in addition to the power of gaining their confidence, had knowledge and tact enough to render them real aid in making selections."
—Samuel S. Green

[from Sensational Fiction in Public Libraries, Library Journal 4, no. 9 (1879): 345-355, 352.]

Anita C. Prieto

Anita C. Prieto was born in New Orleans, Louisiana, and now lives in Metairie. She has a Bachelor of Science degree in Education and a M.Ed. in Educational Administration from Louisiana State University. Her doctorate (Ed.D.) is from the University of New Orleans. Anita's professional life (33 years) was spent in the Orleans Parish School System where she worked as a classroom teacher, television teacher, school principal, and acting area superintendent. She is now retired and writing full-time. Her favorite pastimes include traveling, reading, gardening, and playing Mah-Jongg with friends. Anita is also the author of *P is for Pelican: A Louisiana Alphabet*.

Renée Graef

Renée Graef is well known as the illustrator for the "Kirsten" books in the *American Girl* children's book collection. She has also illustrated many books in the *My First Little House* series with HarperCollins. Renée received her Bachelor's degree in Art from the University of Wisconsin-Madison. Her first book with Sleeping Bear Press was *B is for Badger: A Wisconsin Alphabet*. Renée lives in Cedarburg, Wisconsin with her family.